Basic Idioms In American English

BOOK 1

HUBERT H. SETZLER, JR.

SRA®
SCIENCE RESEARCH ASSOCIATES, INC.
Chicago, Palo Alto, Toronto, Henley-on-Thames, Sydney
A Subsidiary of IBM

شناسنامه کتاب

نام کتاب : Basic Idioms In American English Book 1

تیراژ و نوبت چاپ : چاپ اول ۵۰۰۰ جلد

لیتوگرافی : درخشان

چاپ و صحافی : [illegible]

ناشر : انتشارات جنگل (Jungle publication - Iran - Tehran)

Illustrations by Sedonia Champlain
Cover design by Caroff/Reiken

Published by
Science Research Associates, Inc.
155 North Wacker Drive
Chicago, Illinois 60606

ISBN: 0-574-16012-4

Printed in the United States of America

Preface

This is the first of a two-book series entitled *Basic Idioms in American English*. They are intended for students of English as a foreign language. Idioms are a constant source of difficulty for non-native speakers of English since direct translations often prove nonsensical and misleading. However, mastery of the most commonly used idiomatic expressions is essential for natural, everyday communication. The idioms contained in these two books have been selected for their high frequency and are constantly used by most Americans in their daily lives. Each lesson includes dialogues based on actual conversations, interviews, recorded by the author. These interviews accurately reflect the living language of Americans of all ages and walks of life.

The books are divided into modules of four lessons each. Each lesson begins with a dialogue which introduces the new idioms in context. This is followed by an alphabetically-arranged list of all new idioms with their respective definitions and two or more sample sentences. Then the student is asked to use the idioms in a variety of exercises.

Each module is a self-contained learning unit, that is, the student does not need to learn the first module in order to study the second one. The modules are independent, as are the lessons, but they are presented in a suggested progression. Teachers and learners of English can easily adapt the lessons to their own curriculum, interests, or individual needs.

Book 2 is a continuation of Book 1 in all respects. Its seven modules include PEOPLE, THINKING, INFORMATION PLEASE, PROBLEMS AND SOLUTIONS, FEELINGS, HUMAN RELATIONSHIPS, and DOING.

Only extensive drill and practice will bring complete mastery of the many idiomatic expressions of the English language. Our goal in these books has been to make this task enjoyable and rewarding.

Contents

MODULE 1 Come To Your Senses

Lesson 1: How We See Things

Interview

The interviewer goes into Ted Long's camera shop. He saw an ad in the newspaper for a new 35 mm camera at Long's Camera World.

Int: Good morning, Ted. I saw your ad in the paper. I want to **see about** a new camera.

Ted: Fine. **Look at** this one. It's a great camera. It just came from Japan.

Int: Oh, yes. It's really nice. May I **take a picture**? I'd like to see how it works.

Ted: Sure. Just **watch out for** the flash. You're looking right into it.

Int: Yes. I guess I don't know much about cameras. I'm going to **look to** you for advice.

Ted: Fine. I'll be glad to help.

Look at *to watch, to examine*

Children are very curious. They **look at** everything.

Look at me! I'm going to jump in the water.

May I **look at** that calculator? I need to buy one.

Look to *to expect, to rely on*

Students **look to** the teacher for help.

John **looks to** the future. He expects to be successful.

See about *to investigate, to attend to*

Linda went to **see about** a new job.

I don't have time to put gas in the car today. I'll **see about** it tomorrow.

Take a picture (of) *to photograph*

Quick! **Take a picture** of that beautiful sunset!

I **took a picture** of my dog yesterday.

Watch out (for) *to be on the alert for, to guard against*

At the seashore we must **watch out for** sunburn.

Watch out! That cat may scratch you.

Exercise 1

Select the correct definition for the boldface phrase.

1. **Look at** that sports car.
   a. Watch
   b. Be on guard against
   c. Photograph
2. **Take a picture of** me.
   a. Watch
   b. Be on guard against
   c. Photograph
3. **Watch out for** that dog.
   a. Watch
   b. Be on guard against
   c. Photograph
4. **Look to** your teacher for help.
   a. Rely on
   b. Attend to
   c. Investigate
5. Did you **see about** buying a new TV?
   a. Rely upon
   b. Gaze upon
   c. Investigate

Exercise 2

Fill in the blanks with the correct idiom.

Take a picture
Look at
Look to
Watch out for
See about

1. George was driving on the highway. His wife said, "________________ speeding cars."
2. Jose works very hard. He wants to be successful. He said, "I'm ________ ing ______ the future. That's why I work so hard."
3. Mr. Sekino wants to buy a new TV. He said, "I want to ________________ several models before I buy a new television set."
4. Mr. Sekino went to the store. He wanted to ________________ buying a new TV
5. Meg is a photographer. She saw an interesting flower. She said, "I want to ________________ of that flower."

MODULE 1 Come To Your Senses

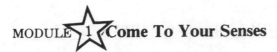

Lesson 2: Asking for Advice

Interview

The interviewer goes to a travel agency. He is planning a vacation. He is speaking to Judy Davis, one of the travel agents.

Ms. Davis: What about the Dalmatian coast? It's beautiful.

Int: Yes, I've **heard of** it. It's part of Yugoslavia, isn't it?

Ms. Davis: That's right. I went there last year. It was wonderful.

Int: Really? So you think my wife and I would like the Dalmatian coast.

Ms. Davis: Yes, absolutely. After our trip, my husband and I **talked about** it for weeks.

Int: Do you have any special tours or information that I could look at?

Ms. Davis: Yes. We have several complete vacation packages. You should **speak to** our tour director.

Int: Yes, I'd like to **ask for** his advice also.

Ms. Davis: Fine. Just wait a minute. I'll ask him to come and **talk about** it with you.

Int: Yes, I would like to **listen to** him before I decide.

Ask for *to request*

My son **asked for** a sandwich. My daughter **asked** me **for** a glass of milk.

Hear of *to know about, to have knowledge of*

Who is Willie Priest? I never **heard of** him.

If you **hear of** a cheap apartment for rent, let me know.

Listen to *to hear, to pay attention, to heed, to mind*

Listen to the sound of the rain.

Eric is in trouble. He did not **listen to** his mother.

Speak to *to converse with, to talk with*

I shall **speak to** my teacher about this assignment.

She speaks English well. Why don't you **speak to** her about a conversation course in English?

Talk about *to discuss*

Linda and I **talked about** a camping trip. Now we must **talk about** who will go with us.

Exercise 1

Select the correct definition for the boldface word or phrase.

1. When you want to leave class early, you should **request** permission.
   a. listen to
   b. ask for
   c. talk about
2. When you need advice, you should **pay attention** to your father.
   a. listen to
   b. speak to
   c. hear of
3. When you can't find the answer, you should **talk with** your teacher about it.
   a. hear of
   b. talk about
   c. speak to
4. When you have a problem, you should **discuss** it with your best friend.
   a. ask for
   b. talk about
   c. speak to
5. Jane knows about the new restaurant, but Jim **knew about** it first.
   a. listened to
   b. heard of
   c. asked for

Exercise 2

Fill in the blanks with the correct idioms.

heard of	asked for
listened to	spoke to
talked about	

1. Bill was thirsty. He ________________ a glass of water.
2. Who is Dr. Doe? I never ________________ him.
3. That bad boy never ________________ his parents.
4. I need permission to buy a stereo. So I ____________ my father about it.
5. Cherie and Sue ________________ movie stars all the time.

MODULE 1 Come To Your Senses

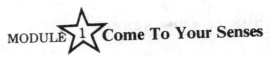

Lesson 3: A Taste of Success

Interview

The interviewer talks with Mrs. Anderson about her daughters Kate and Meg. Kate wants to be an actress, while Meg does not. Kate is ten years old. Meg is seven.

Int: So Kate wants to be an actress.

Mrs. Anderson: Yes. Kate was in a TV commercial last year. Now she's **had a taste of** acting and doesn't want to quit.

Int: I heard Meg was in her school play this year. I suppose she wants to be an actress too.

Mrs. Anderson: No, she doesn't. Unfortunately, the audience **laughed at** her.

Int: Was it stage fright?

Mrs. Anderson: You hit it **on the nose.** She was so frightened she couldn't find the telephone she was supposed to answer. The audience just roared with laughter.

Int: Was the phone in the wrong place?

Mrs. Anderson: Oh, no. It was right **under her nose.**

Int: That's too bad.

Mrs. Anderson: I suppose so. I **smiled at** Meg to give her courage, but she just stood there and cried.

Have a taste of *to have a sample of, to have a limited experience with*

After Tony **had a taste of** city life, he wanted to go home to the country.

My wife **had a taste of** travel and now she wants to go everywhere.

Laugh at *to show amusement, to ridicule*

I tried to **laugh at** Rachal's jokes, but they were not funny.

You shouldn't **laugh at** people who are different.

On the nose *directly, completely accurate, precisely*

Barbara is very smart. She answered every question right **on the nose.**

I made a guess about her age and it was **on the nose.**

Smile at *to express approval of, to show warm feelings toward*

I feel good when my teacher **smiles at** me.

George **smiled at** his little sister.

Under one's nose *obvious and observable, but undetected*

I looked everywhere for my wallet. It was here on the table right **under my nose.**

I should have seen the answer right away. It was there **under my nose.**

Exercise 1

Select the correct idiom to complete each sentence.

1. I arrived home at eight o'clock ________________ .
   a. with my nose
   b. on the nose
   c. under my nose
2. I can't find my pen! Oh, here it is, right________________ .
   a. with my nose
   b. on the nose
   c. under my nose
3. Don't ________________ him. He tries hard.
   a. smile at
   b. laugh at
   c. laugh to
4. Yes, he tries hard. Encourage him. Why don't you ________________ him?
   a. smile at
   b. laugh at
   c. laugh to
5. I can't stop playing baseball. Ever since I first ________________ baseball, I've wanted to play more.
   a. love the game of
   b. played and played
   c. had a taste of

Exercise 2

Replace the boldface word or phrase with the correct idiom.

laugh at
smiled at
had a taste of
on the nose

I **had a sample of** skiing last year. Now I want to ski all the time. I fell every time. My ski instructor didn't **ridicule** me. Instead she really helped me learn to ski. Yesterday I didn't fall. My instructor **expressed approval** of me. I came down the hill very fast. My time was two minutes and thirty seconds **precisely.**

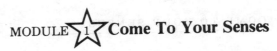

Lesson 4: Think of the Cost

Interview

The interviewer talks to a young high school teacher, Eric Gardner. His father just bought a new luxury car. It is very big, comfortable, and spacious. However, it uses a lot of gas.

Int: What do you **think of** your father's new car?

Eric: I don't like it.

Int: Really?

Eric: Yes, I wanted him to buy one of those foreign cars. I know the one I like, but I can't remember the name. It just doesn't **come to mind** at the moment.

Int: Well, your father did **point out** that the price was low.

Eric: Well, I **came up with** a different price overall.

Int: Oh, what's that?

Eric: I **figured out** that Dad would save over fifty dollars a month on gas. That is, he would save money if he bought a compact car.

Int: Perhaps that's true. Your Dad **came up with** a different idea. He wanted a big car.

Come to mind *to recall, to remember*

I know her name, but right now it doesn't **come to mind.**

Don't worry about it. You'll remember. It'll **come to mind** later.

Come up with *to propose, to suggest, to produce*

Louise is so unpredictable. You never know what she'll **come up with.**

Last week Louise **came up with** a plan to sell insurance to children. Can you believe that!

Figure out *to solve, to understand*

The math exam was hard. I couldn't **figure out** the last two problems. It was impossible to **figure** them **out.**

Lynn was upset about something, but I couldn't **figure out** what it was.

Point out *to bring to one's attention*

The professor **pointed out** my mistakes. He **pointed** them **out** last week.

My father **pointed out** that I should study more.

Think of *to have an opinion about*

What do you **think of** Joan? I think she's very nice.

The company **thinks** a lot **of** their new sales program.

Exercise 1

Select the correct idiom for the boldface word or phrase.

1. Dr. Osawa **has a high opinion** of his new nurse.
   a. comes up high with
   b. thinks highly of
   c. highly points out

2. Some people are hard to **understand.**
   a. think of
   b. point out
   c. figure out

3. I know her face, but **I can't remember her name.**
   a. her name doesn't come to mind
   b. I can't point out her name
   c. I don't think highly of her name

4. Maria **brought the problem to our attention.**
   a. pointed out the problem to us
   b. thought of the problem for us
   c. figured the problem out for us

5. Maria also **proposed** a solution.
   a. thought highly of
   b. came to mind
   c. came up with

Exercise 2

Fill in the blanks with the correct idioms.

figure out · comes to mind · pointed out
think of · came up with

1. My father **brought to my attention** several of my faults, but he also ________________ several of my good qualities.
2. America **produced** a good automobile, but Japan ____________ a better one.
3. My sister **solved** the arithmetic problem, but I couldn't _______ it _______ .
4. What's **your opinion about** my new sweater? What do you ________________ my new shoes?
5. I can't **remember** his address, but his name ________________.

MODULE 2 **Person To Person**

Lesson 1: Meeting Others Halfway

Interview

Ed Burns is a salesman for Kingman Real Estate. He and Mr. Kingman are selling a new home to Mrs. Livingston. They have a meeting with her in a few minutes.

Ed: I can only talk with you for a few minutes. Mike and I have to **call on** Mrs. Livingston.

Int: Is Mike your boss, Mr. Kingman?

Ed: Yes, I **call** him **by** his **first name**. He insists.

Int: The two of you must work closely together.

Ed: Yes. Today we're going to sell Mrs. Livingston a new house.

Int: Really?

Ed: Yes. Last week she **came up to** Mike and asked about the price of our new condominiums.

Int: Do you know Mrs. Livingston well?

Ed: No, I only **know** her **by sight.** Mike is a friend of hers though.

Int: This should be an easy sale then.

Ed: Not really. Mrs. Livingston thinks the price is too high.

Int: Oh. So she may not buy the house.

Ed: Mike thinks she will. She hasn't seen the inside of the condominium. When she does, I think it'll **come up to** her expectations.

Int: What about the high price?

Ed: We'll compromise with her. We'll **meet** her **halfway.**

Call on *to visit*

Friends **call on** friends. Salesmen **call on** customers.

Call (someone) by one's first name *to use someone's name, to refer to someone by the given name as opposed to the family name with the title Mr., Mrs., Miss, or Ms.*

Do you really **call** your boss **by** her **first name**?

Yes, I do. Americans usually **call** people **by** their **first names.**

Come up to *to approach closely, to equal*

Harry **came up to** me and asked for a cigarette.

I hope I **come up** to your expectations.

Know (someone) by sight *to recognize (refers to someone who the speaker has not met formally)*

She is new in our company. I only **know** her **by sight.**

I never met the president of the company, but I **know** him **by sight.**

Meet (someone) halfway *to compromise*

Meet me halfway. I'll pay fifty percent and you pay fifty percent.

We could stop arguing if you would just **meet me halfway.**

Exercise 1

Match the idioms with the correct definitions.

____ meet halfway	a. to visit
____ call someone by his/her first name	b. to recognize
____ know by sight	c. to compromise
____ call on	d. to use someone's first name
____ come up to	e. to approach closely, to equal

Exercise 2

Fill in the blanks with the correct idioms.

call you by your first name
know by sight
meet halfway
call on
come up to

1. Let's visit your parents. Afterwards we can ____________ my parents.
2. If you'll call me Hugh, I'll ____________.
3. I know Mr. Watanabe very well, but I ____________ Mr. Yamada only ________ ________.
4. He'll compromise with you, if you'll ____________ him ____________.
5. That salesman approached me about a new suit. Did he ____________ you?

MODULE 2 **Person To Person**

Lesson 2: Getting Along with Others

Interview

The interviewer is talking to Audra Dixon, a ten-year-old school girl. She has a new music teacher, Ms. Davis. The teacher has come from another town and everyone is talking about her.

Int: How do you **get along with** your new music teacher?

Audra: Ms. Davis? Fine. She's **nice to** me. I like her a lot.

Int: I heard she's very strict.

Audra: Yes, she is, but you **get used to** it. Besides, Ms. Davis is **kind to** all of us.

Int: I heard she was a good teacher. She's really **interested in** music education.

Audra: Yes, sir. She loves music, she's also **interested in** her students too.

Be interested in *to have a curiosity, concern, or fascination for*

Mary Ann's **interested in** Marvin, but he's only **interested in** baseball.

Be kind to *to show someone kindness*

Father taught us to **be kind to** our pets.

Mother's **kind to** everyone. She's a kindhearted person.

Be nice to *to be friendly toward someone, to treat with affection*

We should **be nice to** our new neighbors.

It's hard to **be nice to** a selfish person.

Get along with *to live or work harmoniously with someone*

The two brothers just can't **get along with** each other. They are always arguing.

It's important to **get along with** your mother-in-law.

Get used to *to become accustomed to*

The water in the bath was so hot. I couldn't **get used to** it.

I finally **got used to** using chopsticks.

Exercise 1

Select the correct idiom for the boldface phrase.

1. Barbara finally **became accustomed to** working hard in school.
   a. was kind to
   b. was nice to
   c. got used to
2. That little girl **is friendly toward** that little boy.
   a. is kind to
   b. is nice to
   c. is used to
3. Children often **show kindness to** animals.
   a. are kind to
   b. are indifferent to
   c. are interested in
4. My friend **has a fascination for** electronics.
   a. is used to
   b. gets along with
   c. is interested in
5. Olga **lives harmoniously with** her classmates.
   a. gets used to
   b. gets along with
   c. is interested in

Exercise 2

Fill in the blanks with the correct idiom.

got used to	am interested in
is kind to	get along with

1. Thomas plays baseball, tennis, and golf. He said, "I ________________ sports."
2. Brett and Elizabeth are good friends. Elizabeth said, "Brett and I ________________ each other."
3. Phil lived on a farm. Now he lives in the city. He said, "It took a long time, but I finally ________________ city life."
4. Our teacher is very nice. She ________________ everyone.

MODULE 2 **Person To Person**

Lesson 3: You'll Get Over It

Interview

Ken Morris is a senior in high school. He just broke up with Elizabeth. He talks to the interviewer about his feelings.

Int: So you broke up with Elizabeth.

Ken: Yes, I did. Now I just can't **get over** her.

Int: I suppose it's very hard.

Ken: Yes, very hard. I **went with** her for two years.

Int: I'm sure you'll **go with** another fine young woman someday.

Ken: I don't think so. I never want to **get hurt** again.

Int: I understand. I **fell for** someone when I was in high school.

Ken: Did you **get over** her?

Int: Oh, yes. It was hard, but I finally **got over** it.

Ken: I don't think I can.

Int: Yes, you will. You'll find a young woman who won't **let you down.**

Fall for *to become infatuated with, to become suddenly enamored of; to be deceived or tricked by*

Rusty said that Karen **fell for** Jorge. Karen really loves him.

I don't believe that. Don't **fall for** everything Rusty says.

Get hurt *to become injured (physically or psychologically)*

Be careful! You may **get hurt** if you climb that tree.

When you fall for someone you may **get hurt**.

Get over *to recover from (an illness, love affair, bad experience, etc.)*

I had a bad cold last week, but I **got over** it.

My fiance left me. I got hurt, but I'll **get over** it.

Go with *to date frequently, to date someone to the exclusion of anyone else*

Helen **went with** Carlos for two years. Now she **goes with** me.

Let down (someone) *to disappoint, to fail someone*

I won't **let** Mr. Sekino **down**. He depends on me.

If you keep your word, I'm sure you won't **let me down.**

Exercise 1

Fill in the boxes with the correct idiom. Use the definitions below.

1. become infatuated with
2. date frequently
3. disappoint
4. become injured
5. recover from

Exercise 2

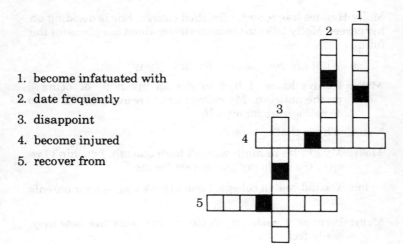

Fill in the blanks with the correct idiom.

get over
go with
fell for
got hurt
let down

1. Vince loves Patty. He really ________________ her.
2. Harold didn't come to my party. He disappointed me. He really ________ me ________ .
3. Vince broke up with Patty. That's too bad. Patty really ________________ .
4. Although Patty got hurt, she'll ________________ it.
5. Now Vince and Patty are back together. They date each other frequently. They are _____ ing ______ each other again.

Lesson 4: Don't Give Up

Interview

Molly Hughes has recently finished college. She is deciding on her career. Molly talks to the interviewer about her plans for the future.

Int: What are you going to do now, Molly?

Molly: I don't know. I had to **give up** my hope of being a mathematician. My college days **are over** and I have to be realistic about myself.

Int: Why is that?

Molly: My grades in math weren't high enough. I couldn't **live up to** the goals my parents set for me.

Int: You did well in college. I don't think you let your parents down.

Molly: Perhaps. I wish they could tell me **to my face** how they really feel.

Int: Why don't you tell them what you'd like to be.

Molly: Perhaps I will. I **used to** want to be a teacher. I think my parents would like that.

Int: It's important for you and them to understand each other.

Molly: Yes, you're right.

Be over *to be finished, to be ended*

When the movie **was over**, we went to the coffee shop.

I wanted to continue our relationship, but Helen said it **was over**.

Give up *to surrender; to renounce, abandon*

After a long battle both armies were ready to **give up**.

Next week I'm going to **give up** smoking. I really want to **give it up**.

Live up to *to guide one's life by; to be as good as*

I want to **live up to** my family's expectations.

Mieko **lived up to** the rules of the school. She made her parents proud.

To one's face *directly to a person*

Ralph criticizes me all the time. I wish he would say it **to my face**.

It takes courage to tell someone he's wrong **to his face**.

Used to — *indicates a habit or action done continually in the past but no longer*

I **used to** go with Helen, but I don't any more.

The milkman **used to** deliver milk every morning. Now we buy it at the supermarket.

Exercise 1

Select the correct idiom for the boldface word or phrase.

1. **I continually studied** English last year.
   a. gave up studying
   b. used to study
   c. was over studying
2. I used to go with Maria, but now it **is finished.**
   a. is over
   b. used to
   c. gave up
3. Don't talk behind my back. Tell me **in person.**
   a. it's over
   b. you give up
   c. to my face
4. Antonio's parents want him to become a doctor. Antonio is afraid he can't **show himself to be as good as** their expectations.
   a. live up to
   b. give up
   c. be over
5. Learning English is difficult, but please don't **surrender.**
   a. live up to
   b. give up
   c. be over

Exercise 2

Match the idioms with their correct definitions.

____ live up to
____ give up
____ used to
____ be over
____ to one's face

a. to be finished
b. to surrender; renounce
c. to guide one's life by; to show oneself as good as
d. directly to a person
e. to indicate a habit or action done continually in the past

MODULE 3 Time and Time Again

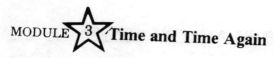

Lesson 1: A Good Time

Interview

The interviewer talks with Jim Marshall, a TV game show host. He enjoys his work and likes to talk about his TV show.

Int: You really seem to like your TV show.

Marshall: Yes, I do. **At times** it's really fun being a game show host.

Int: The contestants must be interesting people.

Marshall: Well, yes. **From time to time** we have trouble with some of them.

Int: Oh? What kind of trouble?

Marshall: Usually, they get very nervous. **Time after time** I tell them to relax. It just seems to make it worse.

Int: What do you do then?

Marshall: I keep on talking to them. I also try to entertain the audience with some jokes and stories. The show must go on, you know.

Int: You mean some contestants never relax?

Marshall: Oh, they all relax—as soon as their **time is up!**

Int: By then it's too late.

Marshall: Right. Someday we'll have to solve that problem. **For the time being** we'll keep on the way we are.

At times *occasionally, sometimes*

At times everyone feels discouraged.

At times it rains for days.

For the time being *for the present, temporarily*

For the time being we live in an apartment. Later we want to buy a house.

Wanda stopped smoking **for the time being.**

From time to time *occasionally, infrequently*

From time to time my parents come for a visit.

I like to go fishing **from time to time.**

Time after time *again and again, repeatedly*

Time after time Mother told me to stop teasing my sister.

The boy continued to get into trouble **time after time.**

Time is up *an allotted period of time has passed*

Larry didn't finish his exam before **time was up.**

We are enjoying our vacation. We want to stay at the seaside, but **our time is up.**

Exercise 1

Fill in the boxes with the correct "time" idioms.

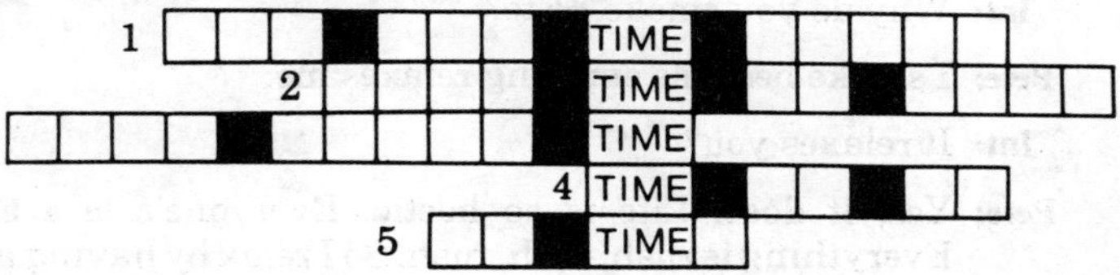

1. for the present, temporarily
2. occasionally, infrequently
3. again and again, repeatedly
4. an allotted period of time has passed
5. occasionally, sometimes

Exercise 2

Select the correct idiom for the boldface word or phrase.

1. **Repeatedly** the child spilled his milk.
   a. From time to time
   b. Time after time
   c. For the time being

2. We all spill things **sometimes.**
   a. time after time
   b. time is up
   c. at times

3. It snows **infrequently** in the southern part of Japan.
   a. time after time
   b. for the time being
   c. from time to time

4. **The time allotted for the exam is completed.**
   a. The exam time is up.
   b. The exam is for the time being.
   c. From time to time the exam is over.

5. **For the present,** I'll study English.
   a. Occasionally
   b. Time is up
   c. For the time being

MODULE 3 **Time and Time Again**

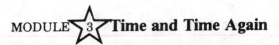

Lesson 2: Quit Smoking for Good

Interview

The interviewer talks with his friend, Pete Vincent. Pete is an insurance salesman who smokes constantly. He is **trying to** stop.

Int: Why do you smoke, Pete?

Pete: I smoke because smoking relaxes me.

Int: It relaxes you?

Pete: Yes, it does. Life is so hectic. Everyone's **in a hurry**. Everything is rush, rush, rush. So I relax by having a cup of coffee and a cigarette.

Int: I've told you **over and over** to stop. Cigarettes can ruin your health.

Pete: I know. **As usual**, I didn't listen to you.

Int: Do you think you'll ever quit?

Pete: I hope so. **Little by little** I'm smoking less every day.

Int: That's great, Pete! Soon you'll be able to quit smoking **for good.**

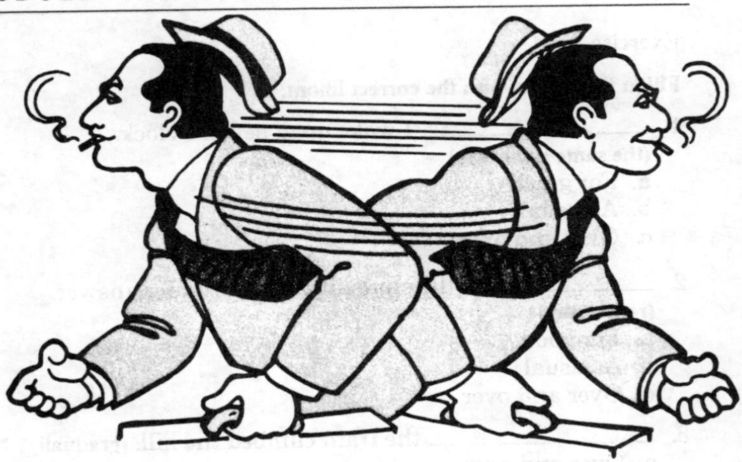

As usual *customarily*

As usual Juanita received high marks in school.

The train was right on time **as usual.**

For good *permanently, forever*

Steve is leaving home **for good.**

Kate broke up with Brian **for good.**

In a hurry *hurried, rushed*

I was almost late for school. I had to eat my breakfast **in a hurry.**

Robert was late for work again today. He's never **in a hurry.**

Little by little *gradually*

Little by little we grow older.

Elizabeth's grades improved **little by little.**

Over and over *repeatedly*

I've told you **over and over** to study harder.

Over and over the child opened and shut the door.

Exercise 1

Fill in the blanks with the correct idiom.

1. ________________ I woke up at seven o'clock. **(the same as always)**
   a. For good
   b. As usual
   c. Over and over

2. ______________ the student gave the wrong answer. **(repeatedly)**
   a. For good
   b. As usual
   c. Over and over

3. ________________ the train climbed the hill. **(gradually)**
   a. Over and over
   b. In a hurry
   c. Little by little

4. I quit smoking ________________. **(forever)**
   a. as usual
   b. for good
   c. little by little

5. We were late for the ball game. We did our homework ________________. **(rushed)**
   a. as usual
   b. over and over
   c. in a hurry

Exercise 2

Match the idioms with their correct definitions.

1. ___ little by little	a. customarily
2. ___ for good	b. repeatedly
3. ___ as usual	c. rushed
4. ___ over and over	d. forever
5. ___ in a hurry	e. gradually

MODULE 3 Time and Time Again

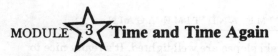

Lesson 3: It's Time to Learn to Ski

Interview

Pat Hale is learning to ski. Skiing is becoming a very popular sport in the United States. Pat talks about his skiing experiences.

Int: How do you like skiing, Pat?

Pat: I love it. **All my life** I wanted to learn to ski. Finally I took lessons last year.

Int: I suppose skiing's easy for you.

Pat: No, sir! I thought I'd never stop falling down. Then **all of a sudden** I started skiing much better.

Int: I see. Do you ski often?

Pat: Every chance I get. On weekends I ski **all day long.** Sometimes I even ski **at night.**

Int: That sounds great.

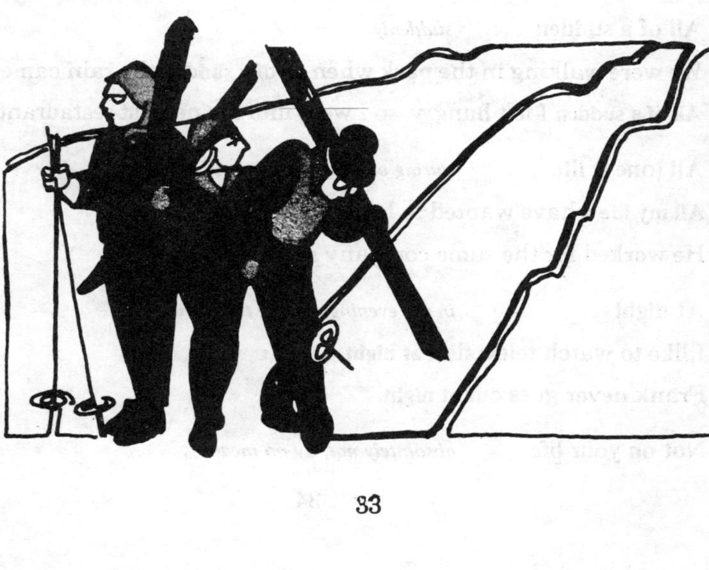

Pat: Oh, yes. The ski slopes are well lighted. It's really nice to ski **at night**. Why don't you learn to ski?

Int: **Not on your life**! I know I'd break my leg!

All day long *throughout the entire day*

All day long Harry worked on his car.

We started in the morning and fished **all day long.**

All of a sudden *suddenly*

We were walking in the park when **all of a sudden** the rain came.

All of a sudden I felt hungry, so I went into the nearest restaurant.

All (one's) life *during one's entire lifetime*

All my life I have wanted to be an astronaut.

He worked for the same company **all his life.**

At night *in the evening, during the night*

I like to watch television **at night.**

Frank never goes out **at night.**

Not on your life *absolutely not, by no means*

Would you like to eat American food forever? **Not on your life!**

Not on your life would I buy that old car!

Exercise 1

Read the passage. Substitute the correct idiom for the boldface word or phrases.

all day long
all of a sudden
at night
all my life
not on your life

During the evening the old man watched TV with his wife. He was tired. He worked hard **throughout the entire day. Suddenly** he said, "**During my entire life** I wanted a motorcycle. I know I'm usually tired, but I'd like to ride a motorcycle in the evenings." "**Absolutely not,**" said his wife. You would certainly kill yourself!"

Exercise 2

Select the correct idiom for the boldface word or phrase.

1. My father and I work in the same plant. My father works during the day, but I work **during the night.**
   a. all my life
   b. all of a sudden
   c. at night

2. Maria wanted to be a movie star **during her entire life.**
   a. not on her life
   b. all her life
   c. all day long

3. My mother looks after the children **throughout the entire day.**
   a. all her life
   b. all day long
   c. all of a sudden

4. **By no means** would I eat raw fish!
   a. All of a sudden
   b. All my life
   c. Not on your life

5. The baby was asleep. **Suddenly,** she woke up.
   a. All of a sudden
   b. All of her life
   c. All day long

MODULE 3 **Time and Time Again**

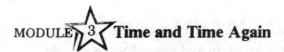

Lesson 4: Going to School

Interview

The interviewer talks with Mrs. Neel, a forty-three-year-old woman who goes to college. She is happy about being in college at last.

Int: How do you feel about **being in school** after so long?

Mrs. Neel: I love it. I always wanted to **go to college** when I was younger.

Int: Why didn't you **go to college** then?

Mrs. Neel: Oh, the usual reasons. I got married and had two children.

Int: I see. How do your children feel about your **going to college** now?

Mrs. Neel: They think it's great. The children even **made room for** my desk in the den. Now I have a place to study at home, too. It's **right here** in the den.

Int: Did it scare you a little to go back to school?

Mrs. Neel: Yes, it really did. I hated to answer questions **in front of** the class. Now I'm used to it. I even like it.

Be in school *to attend school*

My son **has been in school** for three years.

Sally doesn't have a job. She's **in school.**

Go to college *to attend college*

I want to **go to college** when I'm older.

Mr. Yamamoto and Mr. Osawa **went to college** at the same time. They were classmates.

In front of *in the presence of*

You must be careful about what you say **in front of** the children.

I can't believe you said that **in front of** me.

Make room for *to accommodate, to create space for*

Elizabeth wants us to **make room for** Ed in our club.

Move over. **Make room for** me on the couch.

Right here/there *exactly here/there*

Sit **right here** while I make some tea.

I can't find my keys. I'm sure I left them **right there.**

Exercise 1

Select the correct idiom for the words in boldface.

1. My little girl is six years old. She **attends school** this year.
   a. is in school
   b. is in front of school
   c. makes room for school
2. My son will **attend the university** in the fall.
   a. make college
   b. be in school
   c. go to the university
3. Don't eat candy **in the presence of** those children.
   a. right here
   b. right there
   c. in front of
4. My mother **created a space** in my room for a TV set.
   a. made room
   b. in front of
   c. right here
5. Please make room for my desk **exactly there.**
   a. in front of
   b. right here
   c. right there

Exercise 2

Complete the sentences under the pictures.

The teacher is __________
__________.

John is in school. He __________.
Linda is in school. She __________.
Roger is in school. He __________.

Students, please make
__________.

The ______ is right here. The ______
is right there.

MODULE 4 **Start To Finish**

Lesson 1: Keep on Trying

Interview

The interviewer talks with Gloria Bingham, a college student. She wants her father to buy her a car.

Int: **Were you able to** convince your father to buy you a car?

Gloria: Well, I **was about to** speak to him this afternoon, but he didn't come home in time.

Int: Why not?

Gloria: You won't believe this! He **was going to** come home at one o'clock, but his car broke down.

Int: That's too bad. It's a bad time to talk to him about a car, too.

Gloria: Absolutely. I'll have to **put off** getting a car this week. However, I'm not giving up. I'll **keep on** trying to talk to him about that car.

Be able to *to have sufficient ability to do something*

Harry **was able to** pick up the heavy chair.

Tom **is able to** remain calm in dangerous situations.

Be about to *to be ready or prepared to do something*

I **was about to** go to the store when you came by.

Were you about to eat dinner? I don't want to interrupt your meal.

Be going to *indicates indefinite future intent or expectation*

I'm **going to** help you this afternoon.

Are you **going to** read this book?

Keep on *to continue*

When is inflation going to stop? It seems to **keep on** rising.

Even if you fail, you should **keep on** trying.

Put off *to postpone, to delay*

I **put off** my dental appointment until next week.

Do your homework. Don't **put** if **off** any longer.

Exercise 1

Fill in the boxes to construct the idioms. Use the definitions below.

1. to have sufficient ability
2. to continue
3. to be ready, to be prepared
4. to postpone, to delay
5. used to indicate indefinite future intent or expectation

Exercise 2

Fill in the blanks with the correct idiom.

put off
am going to
was about to
was able to
keep on

1. The little child ____________________ write her name.
2. The professor ____________________ the exam until next week.
3. I want you to ____________________ trying to learn English.
4. I ____________________ go to sleep, when the doorbell rang.
5. I ____________________ the movies this afternoon.

MODULE 4 Start to Finish

Lesson 2: Getting Rid of a Problem

Interview

Mrs. Salt, a housewife, discusses the problem of keeping house. Her complaints are common ones in America.

Mrs. Salt: Sometimes I hate to **keep house.**

Int: Why is that? Don't your children **help out**?

Mrs. Salt: No, not really. That's only part of the problem. They collect so much junk I can't stand it. I try to **get rid of** it all the time.

Int: Won't they let you **throw** it **away**?

Mrs. Salt: Heavens, no! It's important to them. The problem is that I can't make room for all that stuff.

Int: When I was young, I liked to collect things too.

Mrs. Salt: So did I. But look at this. My son keeps his old tennis shoes even after he **wore** them **out**.

Get rid of *to become free of*

This big car uses too much gas. I want to **get rid of** it and buy a compact car.

Everything seems all right. But I can't **get rid of** the feeling that something is wrong.

Help out *to assist with a problem*

I have too much work to do. I need someone to **help** me **out.**

Angela's husband **helps out** around the house. He cuts the grass, takes out the garbage, and often washes dishes.

Keep house *to do the work necessary for running a home, i.e., cleaning, cooking, washing, and so on*

Some people like to **keep house.** Others prefer to work with a company or in business.

In today's world the whole family must help **keep house.**

Throw away *to discard*

This shirt is old and torn. I'm going to **throw** it **away.**

Don't **throw away** that old TV. I'll try to repair it.

Wear out *to make or become unusable through heavy use*

The little boy is very active. His clothes are usually ruined. He **wears them out** very quickly.

This air conditioner is no good any more. It's completely **worn out.**

Exercise 1

Select the correct idiom for the word or phrase.

1. This TV **has become unusable.**
   a. got rid of
   b. is worn out
   c. helped out
2. I do not like to **do the work necessary for running a home.**
   a. help out
   b. throw away things
   c. keep house
3. I wish you would **assist me** for a while.
   a. help me out
   b. get rid of me
   c. wear me out
4. I wish you would **become free of** that terrible fear of animals.
   a. help out
   b. throw away
   c. get rid of
5. Did he **discard** that old coat?
   a. help out
   b. throw away
   c. wear out

Exercise 2

Fill in the blanks with the correct idiom.

get rid of	throw away	keep house
help out	wear out	

1. ____________________ that old sweater. It's in terrible condition.
2. ____________________ that big car. It uses too much gas.
3. In the United States there are many men who have learned how to ____________________.
4. Did you ____________________ those shoes already?
5. When a friend is in trouble, we should always ____________________.

Lesson 3: Coming Back Home

Interview

The interviewer greets an old friend, John Eggert. John is a consultant and must travel a great deal.

Int: Hello, John. It's good to see you. When did you **get home**?

John: I **arrived at** the airport this afternoon. My wife picked me up.

Int: I know the children must be glad to see you.

John: Yes, I missed them too. I couldn't wait to **come back** home for the weekend.

Int: There's a party at the Hale's tomorrow night. Would you and Nancy like to **come along** with us?

John: Thanks just the same. Nancy and I are planning a quiet weekend with the children. I have to **be back** in Washington in a few days.

Int: Of course. I understand.

Arrive at *to reach a particular place, goal, or idea*

We **arrived at** the train station at nine o'clock.

Finally the group **arrived at** a decision that was good for everyone.

Be back *to have returned*

Right now Gloria is in school. She'll **be back** at three o'clock.

I worked late yesterday, but I **was back** in time for dinner.

Come along *to accompany*

Hey, Chuck! **Come along** with us to the baseball game.

Make room in the car for the dog. He wants to **come along.**

Come back *to return*

Every year my son **comes back** home for the holidays.

Come back to see us when you can.

Get home *to return home*

Traveling salesmen **get home** whenever they can.

I usually **get home** around five o'clock every day.

Exercise 1

Match the idioms with their definitions.

_____ come along   a. to return home

_____ get home   b. to accompany

_____ be back   c. to return

_____ come back   d. to have returned

_____ arrive at   e. to reach a particular place, goal, or idea

Exercise 2

Select the correct idiom for the boldface word or phrase.

1. I'm going to the movies, but I'll **have returned** by dinner time.
   a. get home
   b. be back
   c. arrive at
2. The two companies finally **reached** an agreement.
   a. came along
   b. come back
   c. arrived at
3. The students **returned home** after school.
   a. got home
   b. came back
   c. go home
4. Please **return** as soon as you can.
   a. come along
   b. arrive at
   c. come back
5. I wish you would **accompany** us to the baseball game.
   a. come along with
   b. come back with
   c. be back with

MODULE 4 **Start to Finish**

Lesson 4: Tired Out

Interview

Phil Rambow is very active in different community groups. As a result, he is often tired out. However, he still has meetings to attend, jobs to do, and places to go.

Int: Phil, you look tired. Did you have a busy day?

Phil: I certainly did. I could **go to sleep** right here in the office.

Int: Why don't you **lie down** then?

Phil: I'd love to, but I have a Boy Scout meeting this evening at seven o'clock. I'm a scout master, you know.

Int: Oh, I forgot. Well, at least you can **sit down** for a while.

Phil: No, you **take a seat**. If I sit down, I'll never get up.

Int: Phil, you just do too much. You've got to take it easy.

Phil: You're right. Well, there's nothing special for tomorrow. Perhaps I'll **stay in bed** and sleep late.

Go to sleep *to sleep, to start to sleep*

You look so tired. Why don't you go to the bedroom and **go to sleep?**

The baby cried all night. He just couldn't **go to sleep.**

Lie down *to recline, take a lying position*

I have a headache. I think I'll **lie down** for a while.

Tell the dog to **lie down.** He keeps bothering our guests.

Sit down *to take a sitting position (after standing)*

Please **sit down,** Mr. Osawa. I want to discuss my problem with you.

We had been shopping all day. It was nice to **sit down** in a coffee shop and relax.

Stay in bed *to remain in bed*

The doctor told my wife to **stay in bed.** She had the flu.

On Sundays I like to **stay in bed** and sleep late.

Take a seat *to sit, to sit down*

Please **take a seat** in the waiting room. The doctor will see you soon.

I'll be back in a minute. Please don't **take my seat.**

Exercise 1

Select the correct idiom for the boldface word or phrase.

1. **Take a lying position** and go to sleep.
   a. Lie down c. Take a seat
   b. Sit down
2. **Remain in bed** until after the doctor comes.
   a. Go to sleep c. Take a seat
   b. Stay in bed
3. Please **sit** over there.
   a. lie down c. take a seat
   b. sit up
4. Don't stand over there. **Take a sitting position.**
   a. Sit up c. Sit down
   b. Take over
5. Please be quiet. I'm trying to **sleep.**
   a. lie down c. go to sleep
   b. stay in bed

Exercise 2

Fill in the blanks with the correct idiom.

went to sleep	stayed in bed	sat down
lay down	took a seat	

1. The boy was tired of standing, so he ________________.
2. I had the flu last week, so I ________________.
3. You look sleepy. Yes, I was, but I ________________ after lunch. I'm fine now.
4. After I went into the office, I ________________.
5. The baby ________________ after he drank his milk.

MODULE 5 **Odds and Ends**

Lesson 1: Making Repairs

Interview

The interviewer takes his color TV to the local repair shop owned by Steve Redman.

Int: Steve, my set's broken. I can't get a picture. Do you think you can fix it?

Steve: Oh, sure. I can fix it. I've fixed **millions of** television sets.

Int: Good. I don't know what to do without TV.

Steve: Don't worry. I'll have it working by tomorrow. In fact, I've worked on this model many times. **Quite a few** sets of this type have problems.

Int: Really?

Steve: Oh, yes. I prefer a different brand. Look at this model over here. This is the only kind I sell.

Int: Wow! That's a great picture. Do you have any problems with this set?

Steve: Well, **so far** I've only worked on **a handful of** them. This TV is really reliable. It should give you no trouble **at all**.

Int: That sounds good. Maybe I'll get one in a few years.

A handful of *a few, several*

A handful of good people can work wonders!

I thought I had plenty of money. All I had was **a handful of** change.

At all *in the least, to the smallest degree*

Lois doesn't like her boss **at all.** She thinks he's a dictator.

Do you mind if I talk to you for a few minutes? Not **at all.**

Millions of *many, very many*

I've had **millions of** chances to go to Europe. Yet I still haven't been there.

Mother told me **millions of** times to help out around the house.

Quite a few *more than several, many*

Quite a few Americans speak foreign languages.

Yesterday I bought **quite a few** books on Japanese history and language.

So far *up to now, up to this moment*

Everything is going well **so far.**

So far I haven't missed a single football game this year.

Exercise 1

Select the correct idiom for the boldface word or phrase.

1. There are **very, very many** restaurants in Tokyo.
   a. a handful of
   b. quite a few
   c. millions of

2. There are **many** foreign restaurants in Tokyo.
   a. a handful of
   b. quite a few
   c. millions of

3. There are **several** expensive French restaurants in Tokyo.
   a. a handful of
   b. quite a few
   c. millions of

4. **Up to now** millions of people have visited the United States.
   a. At all
   b. So far
   c. As usual

5. Do you mind if I smoke? No, not **in the least.**
   a. at all
   b. so far
   c. all in all

Exercise 2

Complete the following sentences with the correct idioms.

1. Have you seen many John Wayne movies?

   Yes, I've seen ________________ them. (very many)

   Yes, I've seen ________________ of them. (more than several)

   No, I've only seen ________________ them. (a few)

2. That's all right. It's OK.

   You're right. It doesn't matter ________________ . (in the least)

3. Up to now, everything's all right.

   Yes, ________________ , so good. (up to now)

MODULE 5 Odds and Ends

Lesson 2: You Never Had it so Good

Interview

The interviewer walks into the room while Cheryl is playing the piano. She is very good.

Int: Cheryl, you certainly **are good at** playing the piano. That's a lovely song too.

Cheryl: Thank you. I'm glad you liked it. I have a **good time** playing the piano.

Int: How long have you been playing?

Cheryl: I've been studying the piano for ten years, since I was nine years old.

Int: **For goodness sake!** I didn't know that. Ten years!

Cheryl: Oh, yes. Learning to play the piano takes a lot of work. But it's all **to the good.**

Int: **To the good?** Do you make money playing the piano?

Cheryl: I didn't mean it that way, but I do make money sometimes.

Int: How?

Cheryl: I play at wedding receptions or at parties. I get paid for doing what I like to do. I **never had it so good.**

Be good at *to have a skill for*

Norman **is good at** fixing electronic equipment.

Some people **are** really **good at** learning languages.

For goodness sake! *(an exclamation of surprise or impatience)*

Hurry up! We're going to be late, **for goodness sake.**

For goodness sake! You certainly have gained weight.

Good time *an enjoyable occasion, a happy time; an opportune time*

All of us had a **good time** at Joan's party.

This is a **good time** for us to go on a vacation. All of our work is done.

Never had it so good *to be better off*

After I got a raise, I could pay all of my old bills. Life is easy now. I **never had it so good.**

Don't complain about high prices and inflation. You **never had it so good.**

To the good *indicates the amount of profit*

After I sold my house I came out $5,000 **to the good.**

I know how much I started with. After the poker game I was about ten dollars **to the good.**

Exercise 1

Fill in the boxes with the correct idioms. Use the definitions listed below.

1. to be better off economically
2. to have a skill for
3. an enjoyable occasion
4. an exclamation of surprise
5. indicates the amount of profit

Exercise 2

Fill in the blanks with the correct idiom.

1. Norman is ______________ swimming.
   a. good at
   b. to the good
   c. good time
2. John! Come here, ______________!
   a. to the good
   b. never had it so good
   c. for goodness sake
3. I just got a raise. I ______________.
   a. to the good
   b. never had it so good
   c. for goodness sake
4. What a wonderful restaurant! I'm having ______________.
   a. to the good
   b. a good time
   c. never had it so good
5. After expenses I was only ten dollars ______________.
   a. to the good
   b. a good time
   c. never had it so good

MODULE 5 **Odds and Ends**

Lesson 3: Out of Order

Interview

Marion Buckles is a mother with five children. She has had a hectic day. The interviewer talks to her about her day.

Int: I tried to call you today.

Marion: Oh, yes. The telephone is **out of order.**

Int: That's too bad.

Marion: Not really. I can only talk **on the phone** for a minute before I have to **hang up.**

Int: Why?

Marion: Every time I'm **on the phone,** it seems that one of the children gets hurt or something happens.

Int: I can see you've had a bad day.

Marion: The worst! The children got me so confused I missed my dental appointment. I thought the clock said two o'clock. It was actually three o'clock. Honestly, I can't **tell time** anymore.

Int: It can't be that bad.

Marion: Yes, it can. I'm so embarrassed about missing that appointment.

Int: Don't worry. I won't **tell on** you.

Hang up (on) *to replace a telephone receiver in the cradle; to interrupt a telephone conversation by suddenly replacing the receiver*

Wait! Don't **hang up.** I want to speak to Mr. Watanabe too.

I was talking to Mike on the telephone. But he made me so mad I **hung up** on him.

On the (tele)phone *to be speaking by telephone*

Quiet, children! Your mother's **on the phone.**

Many businessmen are **on the telephone** all day. In fact, my boss talks **on the phone** for hours.

Out of order *not working or functioning properly*

Don't put your money in that vending machine. The sign says "**out of order.**"

Everytime I use that pay telephone it's **out of order.**

Tell on *to inform against, to report someone else's misconduct or the like*

Look! You broke my bicycle. I'm going to **tell** Mother **on** you.

Please don't. Please don't **tell on** me.

Tell time *to be able to read a clock or watch, to be able to determine the time of day or night*

I can't **tell time** from the stars. I need a watch.

Children are very proud when they learn to **tell time.**

Exercise 1

Select the correct idiom for the boldface phrase.

1. This soft drink machine is **not working properly.**
   a. replaces the receiver c. out of order
   b. hung up
2. If you don't stop picking on me, I'm going to **inform against** you
   a. tell on c. out of order
   b. hang up
3. When I was six years old, I was able to **read a clock.**
   a. tell time c. on the telephone
   b. tell on
4. I wanted to talk longer **using the telephone,** but I couldn't.
   a. tell on c. on the phone
   b. hang up
5. I couldn't talk longer, because my father told me to **replace the receiver.**
   a. on the telephone c. tell on
   b. hang up

Exercise 2

Fill in the blanks with the correct idiom.

on the phone	tell on	hang up
out of order	tell time	

1. With the new digital watches, it's easier to ______________.
2. That telephone doesn't work. It's ______________.
3. American teenagers talk for hours ______________.
4. After you finish talking on the phone, don't forget to ____ .
5. If you misbehave, someone will ______________ you.

MODULE 5 Odds and Ends

Lesson 4: Shopping and so on

Interview

The interviewer decides to buy a new sport coat. He is talking with the salesman, Craig Rosen.

Int: How does this one look, Craig? Does it look **all right**?

Craig: It's a little too big. You should have **at least** one size smaller.

Int: I hate to shop alone. I like to have my wife **along with** me. She has very good taste.

Craig: I know what you mean. You haven't bought this one **as yet**, so it's not too late to ask her advice. Why don't you bring her here later today. Then she can help you decide on the color, style, price, **and so on**.

Int: That's a good idea, Craig. That's what I'll do.

Craig: OK. I'll see you both later today.

All right *correct, satisfactory, OK*

Is it **all right** if I smoke?

All right, you may smoke, but I don't approve.

Along with *together with, in association with*

Bob went **along with** us to the theater.

I just bought a new stereo **along with** several records.

And so on *indicates a continuing series of others of the same class or type, etcetera*

At camp we went swimming, fishing, hiking, **and so on.**

Let's go shopping for clothes. I want to buy some shirts, pants, socks, **and so on.**

As yet *up to now, up to the present*

I haven't finished school **as yet,** but I will next year.

As yet I haven't received a single letter from her.

At least *a minimum of, at a minimum*

I eat **at least** three meals a day.

You must answer **at least** four of the five questions correctly to pass.

Exercise 1

Match the idioms with their definitions.

_____ all right	a. up to now, up to the present
_____ along with	b. a minimum of, at a minimum
_____ as yet	c. in association with, together with
_____ at least	d. correct, satisfactory
_____ and so on	e. indicating a continuing series

Exercise 2

Select the correct idiom for the boldface word or phrase.

1. That's **OK** with me.
   a. as yet
   b. along with
   c. all right
2. **Up to now** this book has been easy.
   a. As yet
   b. At least
   c. All right
3. Anna bought a new stereo **together with** a pair of headphones.
   a. and so on
   b. along with
   c. come with
4. He ate six hamburgers **at a minimum.**
   a. as yet
   b. all right
   c. at least
5. For lunch we ate salad, meat, potatoes, doughnuts, apples, oranges ________________ .
   a. all right
   b. at all
   c. and so on

MODULE 6 Daily Activities

Lesson 1: Preparing for the Day

Interview

Mary Anderson is a housewife and mother. She is thirty years old and attended an exclusive women's college. The interviewer is asking her questions about how she starts the day, what usually happens, and the like.

Int: What time do you arise?

Mary: Arise? You mean what time do I **get up?** I **get up** around seven.

Int: What wakes you up?

Mary: The alarm **goes off.**

Int: Do you **get up** immediately?

Mary: No, it takes me a while **to wake up.** I lie there for a few minutes and **pull myself together.**

Int: Is this your normal routine?

Mary: Oh, yes. **Day in and day out,** I'm up at seven.

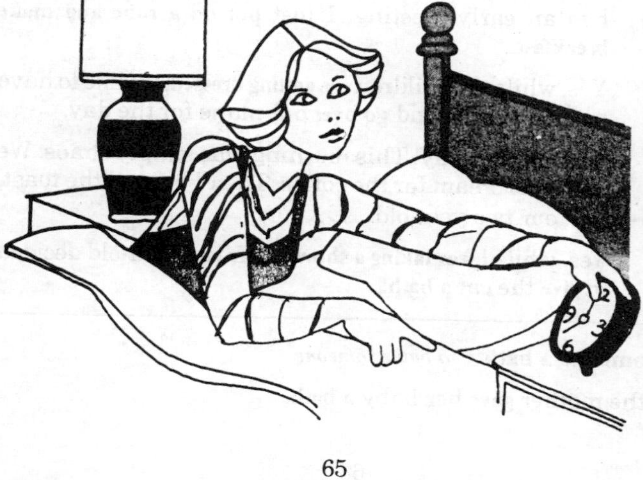

Day in and day out *daily, every day, the entire day*

Ed works very hard **day in and day out.**

Get up *to arise*

I don't **get up** early on Saturdays.

Go off *to ring (said of an alarm clock)*

My alarm did not **go off** this morning and I overslept.

Pull oneself together *to gain control of oneself*

The child cried for an hour before he **pulled himself together.**

Wake up *to awake*

Mary usually **wakes up** before dawn. Then she **wakes** the children **up.**

Interview

Ed is Mary's husband. He is thirty-five years old, owns a shoe store, and is a graduate of military school.

Int: What do you do when you get up, Mary? Do you dress first or have breakfast?

Mary: I usually **get dressed** right away. But sometimes, if Ed has an early meeting, I just **put on a robe and make breakfast.**

Ed: Yes, while the children **are getting dressed,** we like to have a cup of coffee and **go over** our plans for the day.

Mary: Except for today. This morning was simply chaos. We **ran out of** cream for the coffee. Then I burned the toast, and our two-year-old.....

Ed: Yes, while I **was taking a shower**, our two-year-old decided **to give** the cat **a bath**!

Give someone a bath *to bathe someone*

First, the mother **gave** her baby **a bath.**

Get dressed *to dress*

The mother told the child to **get dressed.**

Go over *to review, to repeat, to restuay*

The girl **went over** yesterday's baseball scores.

Make breakfast *to prepare the breakfast meal*

Today Ed **made breakfast** for the whole family.

Put on *to place on oneself (clothes, make-up, and so on)*

I always **put on** my socks and shoes after I am all dressed. I **put** them **on** after breakfast.

Run out of *to exhaust one's supply*

Ed has **run out of gas.** He's also run out of money.

Take a shower *to bathe by means of a shower*

Every morning Ed **takes a shower** before breakfast.

Exercises

1. **Read the paragraph. Replace the boldface word or phrase with the corresponding idiom.**

   Most families follow the same routine **every day**. They **awake** when the alarm clock **rings.** Children often **arise** immediately, but parents will often lie in bed for a few minutes **to gain control of themselves.** On school days, the parents may **rise** first and go **wake** the children. After one of the parents **prepares breakfast,** the family members **review** their plans for the day.

2. **Complete the following sentences using appropriate idioms.**

   a. Some people prefer to ____________________, rather than bathe in a tub.

   b. If you are sleepy, a cup of coffee helps you ____________ ________.

   c. When it rains, you should ____________________ your raincoat.

d. When you are putting on your clothes, you are ____________ ____________.

e. When you ________________ money, you cannot pay your bills.

f. Babies are too small to take showers, so their parents ________ ____________.

MODULE 6 **Daily Activities**

Lesson 2: Transportation

Interview

Helen Fernandez is the head of the data processing department at Berry Cotton Mills. She is forty years old.

Int: How do you **get to work**?

Helen: With the high price of gas, I **take the bus** three times a week.

Int: So you drive to work the other two days?

Helen: I usually **share a ride** with my neighbor, Neal. This way we can **save on gas**.

Int: Isn't it slow to go by bus?

Helen: Well, a little. Even though the bus **makes good time**, I have to **get ready** for work about twenty minutes earlier.

Get ready for *to prepare oneself or others for*

Cecilia must **get ready for** work, while she **gets** her son **ready for school.**

Get to *to arrive at a place, event, or activity*

How do all those people **get to** work?

Make good time *to travel rapidly, to make efficient use of travel time*

Although it was the rush hour, the taxi **made good time** between the airport and downtown.

Save on gas *to conserve gasoline*

We can **save on gas** by walking to the store instead of driving the car.

Share a ride *to go to work with several others in the same car, to go by car pool*

Twice a week I **share a ride** with two of my colleagues. We save on gas that way.

Take the bus (a taxi) *to use the bus (a taxi) for transportation*

I can't drive, so I **take the bus** to work.

Interview

Helen Fernandez's son, Jimmy, is sixteen years old. He is in high school.

Int: So both you and your mother **take buses** in the morning?

Jimmy: Yes, I **go to** high school. I **catch the school bus** at the next corner.

Int: Is the bus usually **on time**?

Jimmy: Almost always. I never have to **wait for** it more than five minutes.

Int: Does it **take longer** to go by bus than by car?

Jimmy: Well, yes, especially in my case. I'm one of the first to **get on** and the last to **get off**. The bus **picks up** about forty other kids between here and school.

Catch the bus *to get on a bus, to board*

If I can't **catch the bus** at this corner. I'll take a taxi.

Get on *to board, to enter*

Get on the bus at Oak Street, ride for six blocks, and get off at Sixth Avenue.

Get off *to leave, to descend from*

If you **get off** at Sixth Avenue, you will have only a short walk.

Go to *to attend a school or college, or university*

My daughter **goes to** Syracuse University.

On time *at or before the appointed time*

The class starts at eight o'clock. Please try to be here **on time.**

Pick up *to collect and take someone (usually with a vehicle), to give someone a ride*

The bus **picked up** three more passengers. As I was driving to work, I saw my friend and stopped to **pick** him **up.**

Take long(er) *to require (more) time*

It certainly doesn't **take long** by car.
The bus **takes** a lot **longer** to get there.

Wait for *to expect, to await*

I **wait for** the bus to pick me up in front of the school.
I had to **wait for** my friend for an hour in front of the restaurant.

Exercises

1. Select the correct idiom to complete each sentence.

a. I take the bus to work. The express bus, especially, ___ .
(1) gets ready for (2) makes good time (3) picks me up

b. By going together, we can save money. We can also ___ .
(1) save on gas (2) on time (3) wait for

c. The bus takes too long. I'll have to ______ to the airport.
(1) get to (2) save on gas (3) take a taxi

d. Congratulations, Maria, I heard your son ___ Princeton University.
(1) is waiting for (2) is going to (3) on time

e. See you later, I have to ________________ school.
(1) get ready for (2) get off (3) get on

f. I'm taking the car tomorrow. Do you want me _______ ?
(1) to save on gas (2) to catch a bus (3) to pick you up

g. Harry can't ________________ work on time.
(1) take a bus (2) catch a bus (3) get to

h. You can ________________ across the street.
(1) catch the bus (2) get ready for school
(3) pick up the bus

i. Anne and I often _________ when we go to work.
(1) share a ride (2) get off (3) on time

j. I don't want to walk to work. It __________
(1) takes a taxi (2) takes too long (3) saves on gas

2. Study each picture. Write a short dialogue using the suggested idioms for each picture.

get on, get off, take the bus, on time

A. ______________________________

B. ______________________________

C. ______________________________

share a ride, save on gas, get to

A. ______________________________

B. ______________________________

C. ______________________________

take the bus, take a taxi, make good time, wait for

A. ______________________________

B. ______________________________

C. ______________________________

MODULE 6 Daily Activities

Lesson 3: At Work, At School

Interview

Rachael Lake is an insurance agent with City Life Insurance, Inc. She finished college two years ago. She is twenty-four years old and has risen quickly within her company. Her sister, Heather, is a senior in college.

Int: I would like to ask you both some questions about work and school. Rachael, what are your responsibilities as district manager of City Life?

Rachael: I'm **in charge of** sales for the whole district. I **make sure** that all new policies **are in order.** I also **keep track of** the activities of all sales agents. Sometimes they don't **pay attention** to deadlines. They don't **turn in** their work **in time** for the weekly reports.

Int: You must be very busy.

Rachael: Yes, I am. I work so hard during the week that I never **feel like** doing anything on the weekends.

Be in charge of *to be the head of, to be responsible for*

Since Mr. Hicks is the teacher, he is **in charge of** the class.

Be in order *arranged or done correctly, appropriately*

You should always check your homework to see that everything is **in order.**

Feel like *to have a desire to*

Today I **feel like** working at home.

In time *within the appointed time*

You must come **in time** to talk with me before class.

Keep track of *to keep a record of, to be aware of*

It's hard to **keep track** of all my books and papers.

Make sure *to assure oneself, to be sure, to be certain of*

I want you to **make sure** that all of the reports are done on time.

Pay attention to *to be attentive to, to listen carefully to, to obey*

The best students **pay attention** to their teachers, their assignments, and their parents.

Turn in *to submit, to give completed work to a teacher or a supervisor*

Turn in your assignments before the end of class. **Turn them in** to your teacher.

Interview

The interviewer then talks to Rachael's sister.

Int: Well Heather, school must be easy compared to your sister's job.

Heather: No, it is not. School is a full-time job. I have three term papers to turn in this week. I have to pay close attention to my professors. I have to make sure that I do my homework **right away**. Sometimes I study all night just to **keep up with** my courses.

Int: I thought you were in school only four hours a day.

Heather: Well, yes, but I have to be there on time—promptly at eight o'clock. After class, I have to study. I feel like I can't **take time off** for anything. Rachael, **on the other hand**, can **keep her own hours.**

Rachael: Not really. I have to **put up with** many problems. Just **keeping up with** the paper work is a full-time job!

Keep one's own hours *to arrange one's own work schedule*

Most salespeople **keep their own hours.**

Keep up with *to maintain the same rate of speed, level of activity or growth, often compared to someone or something else*

It's been a bad day. First, I couldn't **keep up with** all the paperwork at the office. Second, the bank called and told me I would have to **keep up with** my car payments or I might lose the car. Then this evening I went jogging with my wife. I was so tired I couldn't **keep up with** her.

On the other hand *a phrase to introduce a contrast for comparison*

I want to go to school in the evenings. **On the other hand,** if I work in the evenings, I would make more money.

Put up with *to tolerate*

My boss at work doesn't **put up with** any nonsense.

Right away *immediately*

I must talk to my boss **right away.**

Take time off *to arrange to be free from work*

I have worked for two weeks without being able to **take time off,** even for the weekend.

Exercises

1. Select the appropriate idiom and fill in each blank.

a. go to	d. feel like	g. take some time off
b. keep track of	e. is in charge of	h. turned in
c. on the other hand	f. is in order	

Bob Samson ______________ five people in the accounting department. This morning Bob didn't ______________ going to work. "I want to ______________," he thought. "Everything ______________ in my department. I ______________ the payroll checks yesterday. ______________, I need to ______________ the new accounts. I guess I had better ______________ work."

2. Select the correct idiom to complete each sentence.

a. ______________ these reports are written today.
(1) Make sure (2) Pay attention to (3) Feel like

b. ______________ these reports. They are full of new information.
(1) Make sure (2) Pay attention to (3) Feel like

c. Finish these reports when you ______________ it. They are not so important.
(1) make sure (2) pay attention to (3) feel like

d. I want to see your reports ______________.
(1) put up with (2) right away (3) pay attention to

e. He didn't finish the term paper ______________.
(1) in time (2) keep up with (3) is in order

f. When I became my own boss, I could ______________.
(1) keep up with (2) right away (3) keep my own hours

g. These new students can't ______________ the rest of the class.
(1) keep up with (2) are in order (3) are in charge of

MODULE 6 Daily Activities

Lesson 4: Shopping

Interview

Carol Schmidt is a salesperson in a small department store. She is fifty years old. She enjoys the different people that shop in her store. Carol has worked here for over twenty-five years.

Int: I suppose that shoppers have changed a great deal **over the years.**

Carol: Yes and no. Shoppers are basically the same. People still **try on** all the new clothes. They **try out** all the new gadgets and sports equipment. And they just love the new electronic things.

Int: Are there many **bargain hunters** today?

Carol: At today's prices? Of course. Typical shoppers will come in and **pick out** what they want. They may take several minutes to **think it over.** Then they will **make up their minds** to buy the item. A minute later, they may well **change their minds** and **put it back.**

Int: Does that kind of shopper upset you?

Carol: Oh, no! **On the whole,** I would rather see consumers **get the most for their money. You get what you pay for!**

Bargain hunter *one who seeks high value at a low cost*

With rising inflation and the high cost of living, more people are becoming **bargain hunters.**

Change one's mind *to alter a decision or opinion*

I wanted to buy the red sweater, but after I tried it on, I **changed my mind.** I bought a blue one instead.

Get the most for *to obtain the optimum amount, value, quality*

Bargain hunters like to **get the most for** their money.

Make up one's mind *to decide*

He couldn't decide between the green car or the blue one. His daughter helped him **make up his mind.**

On the whole *in general*

On the whole, prices are not as bad as we think.

Over the years *throughout a period of years*

Over the years, television sets and electronic equipment have become more sophisticated.

Pick out *to choose, to select*

With so many stereos available, I took a long time to **pick out** the one I wanted. After four hours, I finally **picked** one **out.**

Put back *to replace, to return*

I **put back** the book on the shelf. I **put it back** because I had already read it.

Think something over *to carefully consider something before deciding*

Before I buy a new dress, I **think it over** carefully.

Try on *to test, to try before buying (clothes only)*

Try on this shirt before you make up your mind.
Try it on now.

Try out *to test, to try before buying, to use for a trial period*

Before I buy a car, I want to take it for a test run and **try it out**. You should **try out** anything new before you buy it.

You get what you pay for *value is in direct proportion to the cost*

I bought this inexpensive watch and now it's broken. It seemed like such a good buy. Well, **you get what you pay for.**

Exercises

1. Select the correct idiom and complete each sentence.

a. I have had some ups and some downs, but ________________, it's been a good year.
(1) over the years (2) on the whole (3) change my mind

b. Go in the store and ________________ the suit you want.
(1) pick out (2) get the most for (3) try out

c. I changed my mind and ________________ the red dress.
(1) put back (2) tried out (3) got the most for

d. Before I ________________, I want to try on this coat.
(1) put back (2) pick out (3) make up my mind

e. I used to spend money carelessly, but ________________ I have become a bargain hunter.
(1) on the whole (2) over the years (3) pick out

f. May I take this TV home and ________________ before I buy it?
(1) pick it out (2) try it out (3) put it on

۵۸۰۲

نام : نوشین کاویانی

کد شناسائی بیمه : ۲۶۴۰۲۰۸۰

سریال کد ارجاع (خاص) : ۰۹۳۰۰۷۲۵۵۹

کد ملی : ۰۰۴-۷۷۶۱۸۰-۶

تاریخ تولد : ۱۳۴۶/۰۱/۳۰	جنسیت : زن
نوع بیمه : همکار سازمان	نسبت : همسر
استان : شهرستانهای استان تهران	واحد : شهرقدس
نام و کد پزشک خانواده :	پرونده :
کد تشخیص :	صفحه : ۲۴
تاریخ ویزیت :	تاریخ اعتبار :

مبلغ ویزیت(ریال) :

مهر و امضاء پزشک

۰۰۹۴

مهر و امضاء داروخانه و پاراکلینیک

قیمت (ریال)		
جمع		
سهم بیمار		
سهم سازمان		
پرداخت بیمار		

نسخه پزشک

نام : نوشین کاویانی

کد شناسائی بیمه : ۲۶۴۰۲۰۸۰

سریال کد ارجاع (خاص) : ۰۹۳۰۰۷۲۵۵۹

کد ملی : ۰۰۴-۷۷۶۱۸۰-۶

تاریخ تولد : ۱۳۴۶/۰۱/۳۰ — جنسیت : زن

نوع بیمه : همکار سازمان — نسبت : همسر

استان : شهرستانهای استان تهران — واحد : شهرقدس

نام و کد پزشک خانواده : — پرونده :

کد تشخیص : — صفحه : ۲۴

تاریخ ویزیت : — تاریخ اعتبار :

مبلغ ویزیت(ریال) :

مهر و امضاء پزشک

۰۹۴

مهر و امضاء داروخانه و پاراکلینیک

قیمت (ریال)		

جمع			
سهم بیمار			
سهم سازمان			
پرداخت بیمار			

g. I brought back the TV because I ______________.
(1) made up my mind (2) changed my mind
(3) picked it out

h. I'll come back tomorrow and let you know my decision. I want to ______________.
(1) get the most for (2) on the whole (3) think it over

i. I can't decide between these two cars. I want to ______________ my money.
(1) try on (2) try out (3) get the most for

j. First, ______________ the suit, then make up your mind.
(1) try out (2) pick out (3) try on

2. Study each picture. Write a short dialogue using the suggested idioms for each picture.

try on, get the most for, think it over

A. ______________

B. ______________

C. ______________

bargain hunter, pick out,
you get what you pay for

A. ______________________
B. ______________________
C. ______________________

make up one's mind, try
out, get the most for

A. ______________________
B. ______________________
C. ______________________

pick out, put back, change
one's mind

A. ______________________
B. ______________________
C. ______________________

MODULE 7 **In the Evening**

Lesson 1: Making Plans

Interview

Amy Taylor and Kathy Belli work in a bank all week. They are both twenty-three years old. They share an apartment together.

Int: Have you planned anything for the weekend?

Amy: Yes and no. I'd really like to **go on a trip,** but I don't have any money. You can't travel **for nothing,** you know.

Kathy: I don't want you to **go away,** Amy. I don't feel like staying **at home** by myself.

Amy: Well, okay. If something does **turn up,** I'll just **play it by ear.**

Int: There's a new movie in town. It's a comedy called *Earrings and Tennis Shoes.* Have you **heard of it?**

Kathy: Yes, I have. It's supposed to be very good. In fact, I heard that the theater was so crowded last night, that many people had to **stand up** to see.

Amy: Let's go see it! I've been **looking forward to** seeing that movie. Maybe your sister would like to go with us.

Kathy: Good. I'll call her right now. **Once in a while** she can get a baby sitter on short notice.

Int: I won't **take up** any more of your time. I know how hard it is to get a baby sitter.

At home *at/in one's own home or residence*

Kate and Ray will have their wedding **at home.**

For nothing/anything *for free, at no cost, for no reason*

The grocer gave us some apples **for nothing.** The supermarket wouldn't do that **for anything.**

Go away *to leave, to depart*

Ed and Mary **went away** for a vacation. They went to the mountains.

Go on a trip *to travel*

Jill was planning to **go on a trip** to Japan.

Hear of *to find out about*

I just **heard of** a new Italian restaurant in town.

Look forward to *to anticipate with pleasure*

My wife and I are **looking forward** to the party this evening.

Once in a while *occasionally*

Once in a while I get hungry in the morning, so I keep a candy bar in my desk.

Play it by ear *to improvise, to do something without a plan*

After we arrive in Mexico City, we'll just **play it by ear.**

Stand up *to rise, to remain standing*

It was so crowded in the subway that we had to **stand up** for the whole trip.

Take up *to occupy or utilize time, space, or resources*

Jim's hobby is building race cars. It **takes up** most of his free time. It also **takes up** most of the space in our garage.

Turn up *to appear, to be found, to materialize*

You lost your car keys? Oh, don't worry. They'll **turn up.**

Exercises

1. Use the idiom in parentheses. Make up a sentence to complete each of the following.

a. Bob bought some apples, tomatoes, and pears. He decided to get just one orange. He asked the grocer to give him the orange for free. The grocer said, "____________________." (for nothing)

b. Ben and Tom have worked hard in their shoe store all year. They need a vacation. Ben said to Tom, "____________________." (go on a trip)

c. It was April. Carlo and Anna wanted to plan their summer vacation. There was one problem—no money. But Anna was optimistic. She said, "It will be okay. ____________________." (turn up)

d. Uncle Larry and Aunt Lou bought a large sofa. When the sofa was put in the living room, there was no room for the chairs. Lou said, "Larry, ____________________." (take up)

e. Aunt Lou is having a birthday party for Uncle Larry. It is a surprise party, but Larry already knows about it. Larry told me, "____________________." (look forward to)

f. After the meeting, the two businessmen knew that their business plans were wrong. As the two men were going into the next meeting, one businessman said to the other, "Don't worry. ____________________." (play it by ear)

g. Ron talked and talked. He would not stop talking. Marty was not able to say one word. Finally, Marty shouted, "____________________." (once in a while)

2. Replace the boldface words with the idiom in parentheses for each sentence.

a. When the bus or subway is crowded, a young person will often **rise** and give his or her seat to an elderly person. (stand up)

b. I just **found out about** the final exam yesterday. I'm afraid I'm not fully prepared. (hear of)

c. I enjoy eating in restaurants, but I prefer eating **in my own home.** (at home)

d. Students make higher marks when they write their papers carefully and neatly. "That's true," said Alice, "but it **uses up** a lot of time." (take up)

MODULE 7 In the Evening

Lesson 2: Eating Out

Interview

The interviewer and his friends Tom and Grace Leclerq went to a local restaurant, The Daffodil. The restaurant is owned by Chuck Jordan, a friend of the interviewer. The waiter is a new employee.

Waiter: Please **sit down**. I've **made room** for you near the window overlooking the daffodils.

Int: Thank you. Tom, Grace, I think you're going to like this place. I **eat out** quite a lot and I've never found fault with the food or the service.

Waiter: May I **take your order** now?

Tom: I'd like to look over the menu a bit more ... The roast beef sounds good.

Grace: I **would rather** have the broiled fish. I've been **putting on weight** lately. The fish would be better for my diet.

Int: Grace, you're so slim. You don't need to **be on a diet.** Look at me! I'm the one who needs to **lose weight.**

Waiter: **Take your time** deciding, folks. I'll be back in a couple of minutes.

Be on a diet *to diet, to try to lose weight*

I don't think I'll eat dessert, because I'm **on a diet.**

Eat out *to eat away from home*

With a large family and the high prices in restaurants, we don't **eat out** very often.

Lose weight *to decrease in weight*

Ed loves to eat. It's hard for him to **lose weight.**

Make room for *to create space for*

John had to **make room for** his new clothes in his closet.

Put on weight *to increase in weight, to gain weight*

Since Rose stopped smoking, she has **put on weight.**

Sit down *to take a seat, to take a sitting position*

Please **sit down** and tell me what the problem is.

Take one's order *to note or determine a person's request (in a restaurant or business)*

The waiter **took my order** and disappeared into the kitchen.

Take one's time *to do something at one's own pace or at one's leisure, to not be in a hurry*

Don't eat so fast! **Take your time** and enjoy the meal.

Would rather *to prefer*

He **would rather** eat at home than in a restaurant.

Interview

After the meal, the waiter returns to the table.

Waiter: Was everything all right, sir?

Int: I'd like to see the manager.

Waiter: Er ... yes, sir. I'll get him. I hope everything was satisfactory.

Grace: What **are you up to,** Hugh?

Chuck: I hope there's **nothing the matter,** sir....Oh, it's you, Hugh.

Int: How are you?

Chuck: Fine. And you?

Int: I'm just fine. As usual, everything here at the Daffodil was wonderful. I was just **playing a joke on** your new waiter.

Chuck: Oh, yes. Our new waiter. Let me introduce you Hugh, this is Larry Johnson.

Int: Hello, Larry, glad to meet you. Your service was excellent. I just wanted to tell Chuck how much we enjoyed ourselves.

Tom: That's right, Larry. And Hugh, since you're **picking up the tab,** I think that Larry deserves a big tip!

Be up to (something) *to be in the process of planning, plotting, or scheming*

I don't know where that child is. He must **be up to something.**

Nothing the matter *everything is all right, nothing is wrong*

There's **nothing the matter** with this meal. Why did you ask?

Pick up the tab *to pay the bill*

My company **picked up the tab** for this trip.

Play a joke on (someone) *to trick someone, to make someone the object of a prank (usually considered harmless)*

My brother loves to **play jokes on** me.

Exercises

1. **Substitute the correct definition for the idiom used in the following sentences.**

   a. There's **nothing the matter** with your car.
   (1) a problem (3) something wrong
   (2) a noise (4) nothing wrong

   b. The doctor told Steve to **lose weight.**
   (1) to reduce his food intake (3) to create a space for
   (2) to become heavier (4) to eat away from home

   c. She **would rather** talk than listen.
   (1) pays the bill to (3) prefers to
   (2) does not prefer to (4) takes a seat to

   d. My wife likes to **eat out**, so she won't have to cook.
   (1) to take one's order (3) to dine away from home
   (2) to be on a diet (4) lose weight

   e. **Take your time shopping.** We have all afternoon to shop.
   (1) Nothing wrong (3) Pay the bill
   (2) Be on time (4) Don't hurry

   f. My mother is **on a diet.**
   (1) trying to be on time (3) eating out a lot
   (2) trying to lose weight (4) making room for me

2. **Substitute the idiom for the words in boldface. Put the idiom in the correct tense.**

   1. John was tired. He **took a seat** and relaxed. (sit down)
   2. The waitress carefully **noted our request.** (take one's order)
   3. Since I saw Fred last, he has **become heavier.** (put on weight)
   4. The parking lot was full, but we **created a space for** my car. (make room for)
   5. My wife **paid the bill** for both our meals. (pick up the tab)
   6. The boy **was in the process of doing** something bad. (be up to)
   7. Yesterday our class **made the teacher the object of our tricks.** (play a joke on the teacher)

Lesson 3: Entertainment

Interview

The interviewer surveyed a number of people on the street, at their business, and in their homes about what they do for entertainment. Here are some typical responses.

Int: What do you do to **have a good time**, Mr. Allen?

Mr. Allen: Oh, there's nothing I like better than going to a good restaurant. And my wife and I go out dancing at least once a week. We really **live it up**, don't we, Nancy?

Mrs. Allen: Yes, we do. We usually **stay out** until two or three in the morning. We really **have a ball**. I have to **keep my eye on** my husband, though. He usually eats too much at the restaurant.

Int: Excuse me, sir. May I ask what you do for entertainment?

Mr. X: Who? Me? I guess I like to just **stay at home** and **listen to** good music. I've a great stereo system—great sound. I spend all my money on records and tapes. I really can't afford to go out.

Int: And you, sir, what do you do for fun?

Mr. Y: Oh, I love baseball. I fact, I'm on my way to the game right now.

Int: Baseball is my favorite, too. You know, if this rain doesn't **let up** soon, the game may be **called off.**

Mr. Y: Yes, I know. I'm going to **take a chance,** anyway. I've had these tickets for a week.

Int: Excuse me, please, but you look like an interesting couple. I would like to know what you do for entertainment.

Mrs. Z: Oh, we have different ideas about that. Henry would rather **take in** a cowboy movie and then go for a pizza.

Mr. Z: Ellen **had her heart set on** the ballet last week.

Mrs. Z: Yes, so we compromised. First, we went to the ballet. Then we got a pizza on the way home!

Call off *to cancel*

The officials **called off** the baseball game. They **called it off** because of rain.

Have a ball *to have a great deal of fun*

The children **had a ball** at the circus last evening.

Have a good time *to have an enjoyable experience*

I always **have a good time** when I'm with you.

Have one's heart set on *to want or desire something very much*

Susan **had her heart set on** a trip to Europe, but she couldn't afford it.

Keep one's eye on *to observe or watch constantly*

You have to **keep your eye on** the children at the playground.

Let up *to decrease, to slacken*

If the storm doesn't **let up,** we can't have our picnic.

Listen to *to hear attentively, to pay attention to*

My son likes to **listen to** his stereo. He never **listens to** me.

Live it up *to have a good time, to live extravagantly*

We usually **live it up** on the weekends.

Stay at home *to remain at home and not go out*

Fred and Jane always **stay at home** and watch television. They never go out on weekends.

Stay out *to remain away from home, to not come home*

Mother told me I could **stay out** until midnight.

Take a chance *to risk, to gamble*

There's a fifty percent possibility of rain. I'll **take a chance** and leave my umbrella at home.

Take in *to attend, to be present and watch attentively*

Yesterday I **took in** four different movies.

Exercises

Make up a short story for each picture using the idioms.

let up, call off, take a chance

A. ______________________________
B. ______________________________
C. ______________________________

listen to, stay at home, keep one's eye on

A. ______________________________
B. ______________________________
C. ______________________________

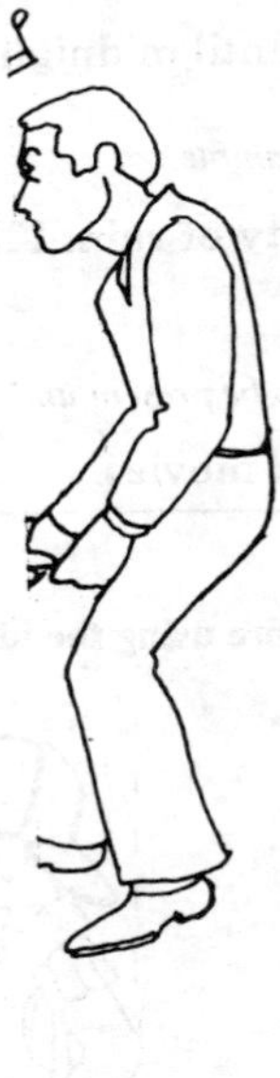

have a good time, live it up. have a ball

A. ______________________________
B. ______________________________
C. ______________________________

take in, have one's heart set on, stay out

A. ______________________________
B. ______________________________
C. ______________________________

MODULE 7 In the Evening

Lesson 4: Preparing for Bed

Interview

Gina Novak is twenty-four years old. She teaches ballet. Today Gina taught classes all day and all evening. She also had a long drive from the dancing school to her apartment.

Int: I'll bet you're glad this day has **come to an end.**

Gina: You're right! **At last** I can relax.

Int: Are you **going to bed** now?

Gina: No, I'll **stay up** for a while. I have some things to do first.

Int: Oh. Do you have a nightly routine?

Gina: Oh, yes. First, I have to **put out** the fire in the fireplace and **put away** my dancing things. Then I **let in** the cat and **take out** my pajamas. After that, I can **get undressed,** and **get into bed.** But I usually don't **fall asleep** right away.

Int: You watch television?

Gina: Sometimes. I usually read a book or just **look back on** my day. I'm **tired out** tonight. The sooner I can **go to bed,** the better!

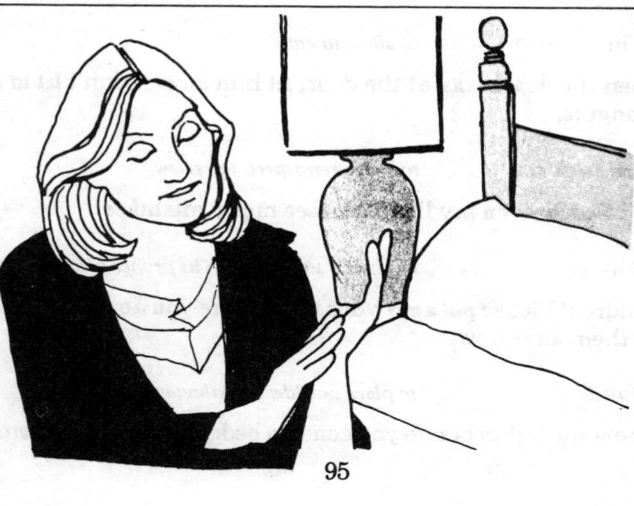

At last *finally*

At last it's time for bed!

Be tired out *to be exhausted*

After working all day, Dr. Davis **was tired out**. She went straight to bed.

Come to an end *to be completely finished*

We liked the movie so much. We hated to see it **come to an end.**

Fall asleep *to go to sleep*

The child was so tired he **fell asleep** in my arms.

Get into bed *to lie down in the bed, under the sheet and blanket*

My dog tried to **get into bed** with me.

Get undressed *to disrobe, to take off one's clothes*

Walter **got undressed,** put on his pajamas, and got into bed.

Go to bed *to get into bed and sleep*

Doris **goes to bed** late every night. That's why she's so sleepy all the time.

Let in *to allow to enter*

When the dog barks at the door, **let him in.** But don't **let in** any strangers.

Look back on *to see in retrospect, to review*

As I **look back on** my life, I can see many mistakes.

Put away *to replace something in its proper place, to store*

Children! Please **put away** your toys before you go to bed. In fact, **put them away** now.

Put out *to place outside; to extinguish*

Put out the lights before you come to bed. Be sure to **put them out.**

Stay up *to remain awake, not to go to bed*

I **stayed up** and watched television until midnight.

Take out (something) *to remove something from, to remove something and place it outside of a container or enclosure*

Before I go to bed, I **take out** my clothes for the next day. I **take** them **out** so that I can get ready quickly in the morning.

Exercises

Make up a short story using the idioms for each picture.

get undressed, get into bed, fall asleep

A. ____________________
B. ____________________
C. ____________________

put out, put away, let in, take out

A. ____________________
B. ____________________
C. ____________________

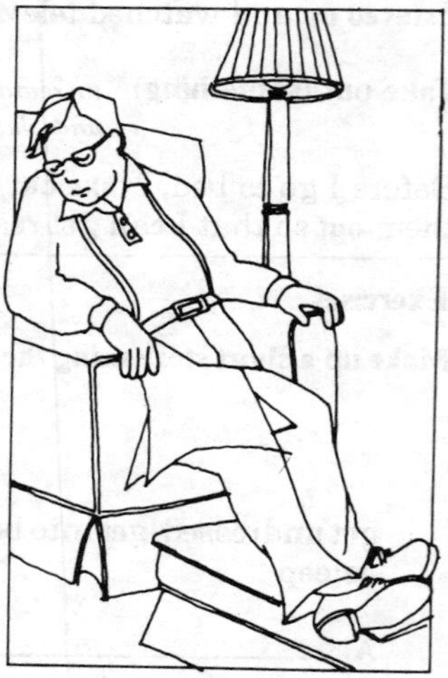

be tired out, at last, go to bed

A. ______________________________
B. ______________________________
C. ______________________________

come to an end, stay up, look back

A. ______________________________
B. ______________________________
C. ______________________________

MODULE 8 Occasions

Lesson 1: Meetings

Interview

Carol Pappas is the new treasurer of the Citizens Park Council. She has just left the monthly meeting of the Council. The interviewer asked her about the meeting.

Carol: It was a typical Council meeting. George **raised the question** about improving the children's playground. That started an argument about how to improve the playground. No one really wanted to **get down to business.** Consequently, the whole evening turned into a big **bull session.**

Int: You mean nothing was accomplished?

Carol: Well, not exactly. Finally, I **had the floor** and told everyone that we must **put an end to** all this bickering. Everyone agreed, but the debate continued. I just **wasted my time.**

Int: Then what happened?

Carol: Well, everyone realized that we would have to **pull together.** The chairwoman, Mary Alice Davis, gave a

speech that **brought the whole thing to a head.** She said we sounded like a bunch of children.

Int: Did you reach a decision after that?

Carol: Well, first we **took a break.** Then we worked in small groups to determine different solutions to the playground problem.

Int: And then you voted on the different solutions?

Carol: Yes, we finally reached a decision. I suspect that Mary Alice worked **behind the scenes** to insure we reached an agreement. Everyone felt that he or she **had a voice in** the final decision. Then Mary Alice **brought the meeting to a close.**

Behind the scenes *.n private, backstage*

Many leaders work with others **behind the scenes** before bringing the decision to the attention of the public.

Bring something to a close *to terminate or end something*

After the lecture, the **professor brought the class session to a close.**

Bring something to a head *to precipitate a turning point, crisis, decision point, and so on*

After weeks of debate, the chairman **brought the question to a head** with the phrase, "Let's vote on it."

Bull session *a discussion without purpose or on trivial topics*

The students like to sit on the steps of the dormitory and have **bull sessions.**

Get down to business *to focus on the task at hand, to begin to work seriously*

Enough of this silly talk! Let's **get down to business.**

Have a voice in *to have some share, say, direction in*

The members of the committee were happy just as long as they **had a voice in** the outcome.

Have the floor ***to have one's turn to speak***

Will you stop interrupting me! I **have the floor.**

Pull together ***to cooperate, to work together***

Unless we **pull together**, we'll never finish this job.

Put an end to ***to terminate (usually abruptly)***

When my mother said, "No," she **put an end to** the discussion.

Raise a question ***to ask or present a question***

Wait a minute, please. John wants to **raise a question.**

Take a break ***to stop for a brief rest or intermission***

There! We finished washing the car. Let's **take a break** before we wax it.

Waste one's time ***to expend one's efforts uselessly***

That old car is beyond repair. Don't **waste your time** trying to fix it.

Exercises

Complete each scene with a sentence using the idioms in parentheses.

a. Jane said that we must all work as volunteers this summer. Pedro responded, "________________." (raise a question)

b. Roberto and Joan worked all afternoon on the school pageant. Finally Roberto said, "________________." (take a break)

c. All of us sat in the cafeteria and discussed how to study for final exams. Lois said, "________________." (bull session)

d. "Let's stop this idle chatter," said Lois. "We have finals next week. That's why we formed this study group. ________________." (get down to business)

e. How could the decision have been made so quickly? David smiled, "Perhaps, ________________." (behind the scenes)

f. John was furious. The decision had been made. He knew nothing about it. John complained, "________________ ." (Have a voice in)

g. Angelo wanted to speak at the meeting. The chairwoman nodded to him and said, "________________ ." (have the floor)

h. The students were tired and the classroom was hot. The professor ended his lecture and said, "________________ ." (bring to a close)

i. Everyone was worried. Then the argument started. "What started the debate?" asked Bill. Nancy replied, "________ ________ ."(bring to a head)

j. When the argument about higher salaries brought things to a head, Loretta said, "________________ .' (pull together)

k. Anna agreed with Loretta. The argument served no purpose. Anna said, "______________." (put an end to)

l. Celia wanted to go to the movies. Sherry was studying for her exams. Sherry replied, "________________ ." (waste my time)

Lesson 2: Parties

Interview

Frank Downs is the manager of a large home appliance store. As a manager of a large store, he often has to attend a number of parties and other social functions. Frank discusses his impressions of parties.

Frank: I suppose I like to go to parties. My wife does too. She likes to get **dolled up** and go out to parties. She says she feels better when she **dresses up.**

Int: Do you like to **dress up?**

Frank: Well, I like to **put my best foot forward,** if that's what you mean.

Int: What kinds of parties do you like best?

Frank: Foreign-food parties. Dinner parties are **the in-thing** right now. I must say I enjoy new foods. Cocktail parties have become so **run-of-the-mill.**

Int: I agree. But there are still a lot of cocktail parties.

Frank:	Oh, yes. There are always going to be cocktail parties. They bore me, but I must admit it's a good way to **keep in touch** with friends.
Int:	Yes, we **take for granted** that the same people will always be there.
Frank:	Yes, but I meet someone new and interesting at nearly every party.
Int:	Didn't you meet your wife at a party?
Frank:	Yes. I met her at a friend's party. We **hit it off** right from the start.
Int:	Did you notice her **right off?**
Frank:	Oh, yes. I saw her the moment I came in. She smiled at me.
Int:	Did she **flirt with** you?
Frank:	Yes, she did. **As usual** she won't admit it, but she did. I'm glad she did.

As usual *customarily, as always*

As usual Frank and Cindy were late for the party.

Dolled up *noticeably well dressed, dressed up*

When Jo Ann gets **dolled up,** she is really beautiful.

Dress up *to put on one's best clothes*

People often **dress up** for special occasions.

Flirt with *to try to attract*

Suzanne was **flirting with** Pierre even before she met him.

Hit it off *to get along well with each other*

Rachel and Brett **hit it off** as soon as they met.

Keep in touch with *to remain in communication with*

After graduation you should try to **keep in touch with** your former classmates.

Put one's best foot forward — *to make the best impression possible*

When you go for a job interview you should **put your best foot forward.**

Right off — *without hesitation, straightforwardly*

When you are in trouble, the best thing to do is tell the truth **right off.**

Run-of-the-mill — *ordinary, mundane*

I was surprised that Mike got a raise and a promotion. He's such a **run-of-the-mill** worker.

Take it for granted — *to expect or assume as true without further investigation*

You can **take it for granted** that Susan will be here.

The in-thing — *the style, action, and so on, that is fashionable*

Disco dancing was **the in-thing** a couple of years ago.

Exercise

Study each picture. Select one idiom for each picture and make a statement that helps describe the picture.

dolled up, dress up, put one's
best foot forward

flirt with, hit it off

right off, run-of-the-mill, take it for granted

as usual, the in-thing, dress up, put (one's) best foot forward

MODULE 8 Occasions

Lesson 3: Uneasy Situations

Interview

The interviewer talks with a number of people about the most unusual situations they have experienced.

Int: What's the most unusual situation you have been in?

Teenage Girl: I think it's this interview. You really **took me by surprise.** I don't know what to say.

Boyfriend: I know how Susan feels. I'm uncomfortable in any **new situation.** It's so easy to **throw me a curve** when I don't understand what's going on. I hate being **in the dark.**

Int: And you, young man. What's your must unusual situation?

Man: Several years ago, I was in a protest rally that **got out of hand.** Boy, that was scary! The police **handled it with kid gloves** so everything turned out all right.

Int: And you, young lady?

Lady: When I met my husband. It was at a party. I didn't know anyone. He **made a fool of me** on the dance floor. It was entirely **uncalled for.** I didn't speak to him for two years, but he kept writing me letters of apology. Now we're married.

Int: What's your most unusual situation, sir?

Man: Well, let's see. I suppose it was when I was drafted into the army. I was always **up to my neck** in trouble. I really felt **out of place.** I just didn't **fit in with** military life.

Int: And your unusual situation?

Teenage Girl: My surprise birthday party that wasn't a surprise. My little sister told me about it. After she **let the cat out of the bag,** I pretended I didn't know about the party. I didn't want to **let on** that I knew. My mother worked very hard planning that party. I didn't want to **throw cold water** on my mother's enthusiasm.

Fit in with *to be in accord with*

Studying English **fits in with** my overall career goals.

Get out of hand *to be out of control, to become excessive*

My wife told the baby sitter that if things **got out of hand,** she should call us at the Johnson residence.

Handle someone with kid gloves *to treat with great diplomacy or tact*

You should **handle Louise with kid gloves.** She can get very angry if you rub her the wrong way.

In the dark *in ignorance*

If Mom finds out what you did, she'll be angry. You had better keep her **in the dark.**

Let on *to reveal, to tell*

I know that Chuck overheard what you said, but he didn't **let on.**

Let the cat out of the bag — *to reveal a secret*

My father knows we're planning to spend our savings on a sailboat. Who **let the cat out of the bag?**

Make a fool of — *to hold up to ridicule, to cause someone to feel or appear foolish*

Are you trying to **make a fool of me?**

Out of place — *uncomfortable, not belonging*

I always feel **out of place** at cocktail parties.

Take (someone) by surprise — *to be unexpected*

We called upon Mrs. Harris to take charge of the meeting. It certainly **took her by surprise.**

Throw cold water on — *to discourage, to dampen enthusiasm for*

Sometimes one thoughtless remark can **throw cold water on** an otherwise pleasant occasion.

Throw someone a curve — *to mislead someone, to deal unfairly with someone*

John didn't exactly lie, but the way he told the truth **threw me a curve.**

Uncalled for — *unnecessary, impertinent*

That last remark of yours was **uncalled for!** Be careful what you say about other people.

Up to one's neck — *overwhelmed by*

Barbara promised to do more and more. Now she is **up to her neck** in work.

Exercise

Select the correct idiom to complete each sentence.

a. That is a terrible thing to say! Your remark was ________ ________!

(1) in the dark (2) uncalled for (3) by surprise

b. You're right, Carol. Henry was ________________ with that remark.

(1) out of place (2) uncalled for (3) in the dark

c. Henry is always trying to ________________ everyone. He's impossible!

(1) let on (2) get out of hand (3) make a fool of

d. Quiet! Here he comes. Don't ________________ that we were talking about him.

(1) get out of hand (2) by surprise (3) let on

e. Well, Toshi knows all about it now. George ______________.

(1) let the cat out of the bag (3) got out of hand
(2) was in the dark

f. Goodness! You startled me. You really took me ____________.

(1) in the dark (2) by surprise (3) let on

g. Magda is a quiet and shy person. She finds it hard to ________________ the group.

(1) get out of hand (2) be up to her work (3) fit in with

h. You two had better stop arguing before things__________

(1) make a fool of you (3) get out of hand
(2) let the cat out of the bag

i. I don't know what she's talking about. I'm completely ________________

(1) the dark (2) out of place (3) uncalled for

j. Jim is very lazy. He had better watch out or he'll soon be ________________ in trouble.

(1) by surprise (3) handled with kid gloves
(2) up to his neck

k. Watch out for that salesman. He's tricky. He'll ________________, if he can.

(1) throw you a curve (3) let on
(2) throw cold water on you

MODULE 8 Occasions

Lesson 4: Social Requirements

Interview

The interviewer discusses social rituals with a young married couple, Kate and Roger Yamakawa.

Int: What's the most important thing socially for a young married couple?

Kate: Well, obviously the most important thing is good manners, whether you're a couple or an individual. Good manners really make a difference. If you **goof up** in most social situations, you'll find yourself **in hot water.**

Roger: I think Kate is exaggerating a bit, but she does have a point. Good manners are important.

Int: So you more or less agree with Kate.

Roger: Yes, you could say so. Another thing that most young couples worry about is **keeping up appearances.** You see many young married couples trying to take part in every social event in town. They seem to be afraid that they'll **rub someone the wrong way** if they don't **take part in** everything.

Int: Are you like that?

Roger: No, not at all. That would be **out of character** for me. I'm pretty **free and easy.**

Kate: That's the truth. Roger acts like he's **on a first-name basis** with everyone in town. It can be very embarrassing.

Roger: Well, at least I'm not a **name dropper** like some of your social-climbing friends.

Kate: Roger! They're not **name droppers.** My friends just like **to rub elbows with** people who are interested in art and culture.

Int: You two aren't going to have an argument, are you?

Kate: No, no. He just **rubs me the wrong way** when he talks about my friends like that.

Roger: Kate has a point. I suppose I **have fallen into the habit of** making fun of her friends. I'll try not to do that anymore.

Kate: Just don't try **to butter me up.**

Be in hot water *to be in trouble, to have difficulties*

If you fail the final exam, you really will **be in hot water.**

Be on a first-name basis *to be permitted to call someone by his or her first name*

Since Maria became a supervisor, she's **on a first-name basis** with the head of the company.

Butter up *to flatter, to seek to ingratiate oneself with another*

Ralph **butters up** all of his teachers. He hopes that will help him get good grades.

Fall into the habit of *to become accustomed to*

Years ago, George **fell into the habit of** smoking after meals. Now, thank goodness, he has stopped.

Free and easy *excessively liberal, very casual*

My friends are **free and easy** with their money.

Goof up *to make a mistake*

Take all the time you want to fix my car. Just don't **goof up.**

Keep up appearances *to carry out a pretense in public view*

George, you don't have to wear a three-piece suit to **keep up appearances.**

Name dropper *a person who mentions the names of important people in order to give the impression of intimate contact with them*

Nancy is such a **name dropper.** You would think she has dinner with the President once a week.

Out of character *inconsistent with normal behavior*

Saving money is **out of character** for most of my friends.

Rub elbows with *to associate with*

Phyllis likes to go to parties where people are interested in culture. She likes to **rub elbows with** artists and writers.

Rub someone the wrong way *to irritate or annoy someone*

When Roberto started acting bossy, he **rubbed Donna the wrong way.**

Take part in *to participate in*

Let's all **take part in** this English class. It's fun to study when we do it together.

Exercise

Study each picture. Select one idiom for each picture and make a statement that helps describe the picture.

Social Scenes

be in hot water, goof up, rub someone the wrong way

keep up appearances, out of character, free and easy

fall in the habit of, rub elbows with, take part in

butter up, be on a first-name basis, name dropper

Index